Authenticity

Authenticity

A Countercultural Perspective

ANITA M. HESSENAUER

RESOURCE *Publications* · Eugene, Oregon

AUTHENTICITY
A Countercultural Perspective

Resource Publications
An Imprint of Wipf and Stock Publishers
199 W. 8th Ave., Suite 3
Eugene, OR 97401

www.wipfandstock.com

PAPERBACK ISBN: 978-1-7252-5196-0
HARDCOVER ISBN: 978-1-7252-5197-7
EBOOK ISBN: 978-1-7252-5198-4

Manufactured in the U.S.A.   04/18/19

To my husband Mike
for his support in bringing this work to fruition

Contents

Introduction

THIS COLLECTION OF POEMS follows the trajectory of the interior journey to the source of our being. It is a journey which calls us to shed all that we have amassed as part of our egotistical nature, in order to attain the wholeness for which we were made.

The poems in this collection attempt to portray some of the salient characteristics of authentic living which is a life aligned to that of our creator. As we journey into the interior life, we come to the realization that the path inward is diametrically opposed to the egocentrism reigning in our world today. This dichotomy is apparent in the reversal of human qualities that are normally cherished in the secular life.

The first section in this collection, titled Paradox, is a depiction of the paradigm shift which is central to the interior life. In order to arrive at the essence of our being, it is imperative that we strive to strip ourselves of our inflated ego. This shedding of all external trappings allows the core of our being comprised of love and all its attributes to be brought to the forefront; for we are made in the image and likeness of God who is pure love. It is only by this self-emptying that we share in the divine nature and thereby uncover our authentic self. It follows that less is truly more and is the norm of an abundant life, hence the title of the first section, Paradox.

The title of the second section, Entreaty represents poems that exemplify the reversal of values in the interior life juxtaposed with those of our fiercely individualistic society. In the milieu where the "I" is celebrated, independence is of supreme importance whereas dependence is synonymous with sheer weakness. Self-reliance becomes the norm whereas vulnerability is taboo. An authentic individual however, recognizes that he or she cannot go through this earthly pilgrimage on his or her own merit and humbly seeks the guidance and help of the Lord. Such an individual acknowledges his or her own brokenness as well as the frailty of the human condition and calls out to our maker for succor. The recognition of dependence is reflected in the second section of this collection, Entreaty.

The third section titled Giving, presents individuals whose lives reflect their inner core of love. Three of the poems in this section, "Where are the Blessings . . .?," "Giving" and "The Gift" are set in India, the country of my birth where I spent the first nineteen years of my life.

Authentic living flows out of a giving of oneself to another. Narcissism has no role in such a life for an authentic life does not hoard its gifts but finds fulfillment in dying to self and living for the other. Furthermore, the vision of one living such a life is transformed. This individual upholds the inherent value and dignity of the destitute and of those who are marginalized. An authentic individual also plumbs the depths of situations which customarily carry a negative connotation, uncovering the blessings buried within them. The final section of this collection, Giving, portrays such a grace filled individual.

The reversal of values is the thread that binds together the three sections of this collection. Authenticity entails the recognition of the source of one's being. It is the trait of one who dares to be countercultural. The benchmarks of an authentic life form a stark contrast to the prevalent norms in our culture and society. An authentic life is one which is dependent on the Lord and which has its gaze and steps turned outward toward the other.

I

Paradox

WHAT ARE YOU LOOKING FOR?

In search of the creative Word
Strip and lay bare the strata that envelops mankind
Devoid of transparency.
Stained, soiled, muddied.
Penetrating the depths
Reaching the core
Revealing the nucleus.

Authenticity
Without duplicity
Love unconditional
The radiance flows.

In your image
In your likeness
Without distillation
It multiplies. It grows.

Its contagion
A blanket soft and secure
Enwraps each being
Spreads its warmth
Envelops your creation
A pure revelation
Of you Lord, the Word, the Creator.

ORIGINALITY

Parched wasteland
Bountiful fecundity.
Aridity unsurpassed.
Geyser issues forth
Inundation of barrenness.

Stunted Growth
Shriveling of foliage.
Scorching heat
Burning incinerator.
Cinders, cinders.

A new spring
A blossoming
New vision.
The carapace is broken
The cocoon is shed.

Breathing free
Streamlined
Skeleton.
Essential fullness
Trueness

DENUDATION

Denudation
Stripping bare
Return to purity
Unadulterated.
Without dilution
Uncorrupted.

Wrapped in layers
Suppression of goodness.
Year after year
The schism grows and multiplies.
The external conditions the interior
Mimicry and falsity, the result.

The barrier is strengthened
But is it authentic?
A response it is to stroke the ego.
Narcissistic, Impressionistic
Genuine? No!

Denudation
Stripping bare.
Reaching the core
Sighting the nucleus.
Authenticity, transparency
No diplomacy.
This is what man was meant to be.

Radiance emanating
Love propagating
Darkness obliterating
The Creator reflecting.

A SMALL VOICE

Keep your eyes fixed on my son
I heard a small voice whisper.
In my brokenness you made me whole
I considered myself inconsolable but you
Instilled in me peace beyond all belief.

I come before you a cavernous vessel
My mind devoid of all thought.
I come before you with empty hands
Longing to be filled.
In my barrenness I stand before you.

A voice rends my interior stillness
It is but a whisper yet sounds like a gong
Echoing through my faculties.
Do you not understand that it is the desert that finds itself in bloom?
In aridity that an oasis is formed?
A parched well that's filled to overflowing?

Eloquence is without merit
Conversation superfluous.
Emptiness is true fullness
Less is truly more.
Silence is cherished.

I am the abundance within you
The Source which makes you whole.
Quell your words, abandon your babble
Be still and rest in me.

You are my vessel
You are my mirror
Live in my presence
And you will be filled.

II

Entreaty

UNION

Bread of Life
Manna unsurpassed
Radiant indwelling
Infusing our being.

Give us the humility to acknowledge
That you alone are perfect;
That in our brokenness we aspire
Not to perfection but to progress.
That every stride forward, no matter how small
And imperceptible is our desire for you.

Clouds grey and blue
Make their dwelling within us.
The recesses of our hearts
Are shrouded in darkness and in light.
Rid us of our self-righteousness
May condescension and judgmentalism
Make not their home in us.

Every dark cloud has a silver lining
The darkest of nights is penetrated
By a ray of light
Showing us the path of hope that lies ahead.
Let pessimism drown in a sea of optimism
With the refusal to give up; the refusal to quit.
To be governed by resignation.

Show us Lord, that authentic union
Is in breaking down barriers
And building bridges.
In finding you in places unimagined.
In the stranger that repels us

In the person right next to us
Close, yet so very distant.
Show us Lord, that it is through empathy and compassion
That we are made whole;
That it is through uniting with humanity
That we find true union with you.

TEACH US TO SEE

Lord, teach us to see.
To look beyond
To look deep
To see with your eyes,
The eyes of Love
A vision of compassion.

To have courage beyond measure
To shatter the grip of fear
Of chastisement
Of isolation.
Break the shackles of habit, of social decorum
All that conditions us
To complacency and stagnation.

You have said "Be not afraid"
May this assurance
Accompany us always
Ringing in our ears
At the center of our hearts.
A soothing touch to gnarled hands
A gentle kiss to a starved body
A smile on a face that knows not how to laugh
A hug that swallows the loneliness
Bringing light, your light into eyes hollowed through endless pain.

Lord, teach us to see.
Teach us to see your many faces of Love.

DISCIPLESHIP

Your light shone on my path
    You asked me to follow you.
        I hopped aboard as one blindfolded
        I let you lead me.
Lord, how far do you want me to go?

I followed you as your shadow
    I heard your voice in time of need.
        I always knew you were there
            When I called in the desert.
Lord, how far do you want me to go?

The journey has been long and arduous
    But I cannot hop off now.
        When I retreated into the shadows
            You drew me out into your radiant light
                Saying, quicken the pace, you can't call it quits.
Lord, how far do you want me to go?

My steps have quickened, I lag not behind
    My ears are accustomed to your call
        I know full well now, I must go on
            Until I give you my all.

ABUNDANT LIFE

You are the bountiful harvest
The infinite geyser
Inundating all barrenness

As a phoenix rising from its ashes
I am reborn
Into a new spring
A blossoming
With clarity of vision.

I see reality anew
Penetrating the surface
Looking past the exterior
Scanning the depths
Multidimensional.
Aligning mind, heart and action.

Though imperfect
Riddled with discord
Stepping in rear motion
You propel me forward.
Your strength
Your love
Accompany me as
Constant Companions.

The cocoon is shed
The carapace is broken.
Breathing free
I experience your fullness.

EQUILIBRIUM

The wheels

Churn

Turn

Spin

Erratically

On the pillow of time

Cast

Into the choppy sea

Tossed

And

Turned

On monstrous waves.

Grappling

With

Greys

Blacks

Punctuated with "What-ifs?"

Recurring theme

Multiplicity of endless scenarios.

Gripped

In the tentacles

Of the octopus

Blood pressure climbing

Mounting

Rising

Migraine

Cold sweat.

Jolted

Lightning strikes

The spokes

A grinding halt.

Stay in the boat

Grab the oar

Follow the course
Don't jump ship.
The compass
Within
Calls out.
A hushed whisper
Barely audible
Yet distinct
Clear
Unmistakable
Rising
To
A crescendo
Gamelan.
A veritable
Tearing asunder. . .
Then
Serenity.
The navigator
Within
Soothes the faculties
Calms the psyche
Stabilizes the physique.
Silence the doubts
Steer
Don't veer
The boat will arrive
Intact
Brought ashore
Amidst
Cerulean waves.

THE PRIVILEGED ONE

Keep your eyes on my son
Let there not be anguish, let there not be fear.
He has cradled you in His arms
He has made you His own.

Give your heart to my son
His gaze is fixed on you.
He has chosen you; He has made you whole.
Keep your eyes on my Son.

Meditate on the wood of the cross
On which hung the corpus of my Son.
The bare wood has no value, it is of no worth.
It is the wholehearted sacrifice of my Son
That has rekindled mankind and given us new birth.

You are the privileged one, the one marked with the cross.
He has given you the strength, He has given you the heart
That sets You apart -
Go forth my child, emulate me
You are my true missionary.

Carry your burden with detachment
Trust in me with abandonment.
Shine my light on those around you
Seize this moment to make me known.

PRAYER OF REBIRTH AND RENEWAL

I am shackled in pain, Lord
My heart and my mind writhe in torment.
I am trapped in the confines of my body.

Lord, in your infinite and unfathomable divine mercy
Cast off these chains, release me from my shame.
The shame which keeps me from the truth,
The truth that beauty is not skin deep.

Show me Lord, the deep beauty within me,
The grace within my soul, the very core of my being.
Keep the eyes of my heart fixed on you,
On your magnificent cross.

Lord, stoop down and bless me in my anguish.
Pour out upon me the grace to see that my pain
Is the way out of this circle of shame
Which haunts me day and night.

Lord, your strength flows through me.
You fill me with restraint and self-control.
Your hands guide me, your feet lead me.
I am filled with your radiant light.
Your presence illuminates me.

I hear you whisper: my child, go forward, be not entrapped.
I have taken away your shame.
You are reborn, you are resurrected!

III

Giving

ACCOMPANIMENT

Rest your head on my shoulder
Let the tears flow.
Lay your hand in mine
Feel the surge -
Strength
Security.
Hear the beats synchronize
Beat as one.
Taste the salt commingle.
I share your burden
I bear your pain.
A kindred soul
Accompanies you,
Walks in your footsteps
Carries the weight.

WHERE ARE THE BLESSINGS. . .?

The wings of the big bird whirring on the tarmac
Set my heart a flutter.
Traveling across these many miles
Expectations ride high.
Meticulously balancing my luggage on the trolley
My eyes scan the surroundings
Melt into a potpourri of alien, impassive faces.
Humanity scurrying helter-skelter
Pandemonium.
Then silence.
An island unto myself
Alienated
Motionless
Apprehensive
Fear -
Not a familiar face in sight.

With leaden feet
I drag myself
Following the figure ahead
Stopping in fits and starts
Until the mayhem envelops me
And the din of horns, vehicles and people
Swirls about me. I am trapped, a prisoner of the chaos.
Panic overtakes me, I look to and fro.
Not a kindred soul, no, not even a wave.
Claustrophobia overpowers me as I weave my way through
The melee. My head swims and the pounding of my heartbeat resounds:
Where are the blessings, O Lord?

I am jostled as I cling to my possessions.
My purse, my pocketbook, my bags.
Gazing fixedly ahead

A sea of blank faces greets me
While the cries of the *rickshaw wallahs* and the taxi drivers
Pierce my ears.
Deafening.
I can stand it no more.
Immobile. Amidst a moving wall of figures
Hemming me in on every side.
Forced back
Toes stepped on.
Struggle to regain equilibrium
Gasping to remain afloat.
My hand luggage topples over the bars of the trolley
Falling onto the bare pavement with a thud.
The pounding in my head intensifies
My knees won't hold me up
My throat is parched.
Everything swims around me. I am about to collapse.
Where are the blessings, O Lord?

I am enveloped in arms smothering me
As my name reverberates.
Through eyes barely open
I see the smiles on the overjoyed faces
Of those who greet me.
I am swept off my feet,
My bags are grabbed,
My arms are free.

The din of the traffic,
The shrill sound of horns,
Vendors touting their wares
Competing to get the attention
Of every passerby.
Animals galore,
Dogs, cows and pigs

Mingled with humanity
Fighting for survival.
The garbage heaps,
The stench that fills my nostrils,
The emaciated young mother,
With hollowed face and sunken eyes
hugs the withering babe
On her waist, pleading for a rupee or two.
My heart is in my mouth
As I cry out
Where are the blessings, O Lord?

An outpouring of emotion.
We're elated to see you
It's been an eternity -
Twenty long years.
Words cannot express our joy.
We sincerely hope you'll relish
The banquet that awaits you!
Everyone's excited and impatient
To meet you.
The house has been humming in anticipation. . .
The joyful chatter, the ringing laughter
The broad smiles, the twinkle in the eyes
Shatter the silence,
Invade my thoughts.
Laughter, joy, largesse of heart and mind
Are these not the intruders trespassing
Into the squalid streets
Spilling over with poverty and desolation?
Strangers in this cosmos of human misery.
My sullen face breaks into a weak smile
As I acquiesce with a nod while
my heart bleeds like a fresh wound.

AUTHENTICITY

I am lifted up in a cloud of hugs,
A goddess to be revered.
Barefooted children
Bow down reverently before me, touching my feet
In a mark of profound respect.
Love and care pervade the air
obliterating the vividly depressing images
dominating my mind.

Cast not your emphasis on the externals,
Let not the horror weigh you down.
Wake up and understand
That every dark cloud has a silver lining.
Grasp the light, live in its glow.
May you be transformed in its radiance
May you be the one to grow.
Bask in the love and sow it freely.
Open your heart in spontaneous appreciation,
Multiply the care you show.
Harbor not the darkness but bathe in the light.
Elusive, wrapped in somber hues
The blessings flow.
Absorb the warmth
Cherish the love
Dispel the darkness
Live in the light.

SWADDLED

Forlorn, dejected he stands
Swaying like a windswept tree
Uprooted
Beaten down in the storm
Isolated
An island unto himself.

The desolate landscape
Is reflected well in him
The icicles on the barren branches
Find their counterpart in his heart
An icebox.
Shunned.

He hears the laughter
It rings out loud
Echoes in the air
Reaches his ears.
Smiles on youthful faces
Warmth in hearts
Gratitude on lips.
The hugs linger
They are loved.
The red suit
Symbol of cheer.

He once was swaddled
Cradled in his mother's arms.
Warmth.
Everything aglow
His heart, a burning fire.
He is stripped
Sapless.

All that remains are embers
Ashen flakes
Cinders.
The cloths are abandoned
The body gone
Solitude
Abandonment
Ultimate sacrifice
Fruit of love.
Dying to self
Living for others.

SAMARITAN

A cry loud and clear
Piercing the stillness.
Deafening
Not to be ignored.
I look, I see
But merely superficially.
With eyes open wide
But in essence closed.
I do not see
I do not hear
I am deaf
To the pleas
To the entreaty
For help.

Is it fear?
Going beyond
My limits?
I have set up
Boundaries
In my mind
In my heart.
I will help
But only to a certain extent.
I cannot go further
It's asking too much.
I've stroked my ego
A purveyor of kindness
And compassion
I walked in the shoes
Of those I visited
At the nursing home
I call myself the Samaritan.

Reverse my mind set

Open

Widen

Encompass

Include

All

Be not afraid

Hesitate not

Shrink not from going the extra mile.

Be the Good Samaritan.

THE FRAGRANCE OF LOVE

The fragrance of Love beckons
It wafts through the air,
A sweetly scented blossom.
Alluring, enchanting. . .

Leave the petals intact
Unlock the elixir
Bottled in the depths.
Let its fragrance linger
Enveloping you
Filling your senses'
Humming its unmistakable melody in your ears. . .
"You are loved!"

See the butterfly hover
Drinking deeply of the nectar.
Treading lightly, oh, so lightly.
Let not your steps descend
Or tread on the thorny abode. . .

Open the doors beyond your confines
Let in the outsider. . .
Share the elixir
Share it freely
Don't hold back.

See the seeds on the thistle
sailing in the wind.
Transformed, inviting
They welcome the stranger
To share in the fragrance.

Limitless
Without boundaries.

There's no dearth of *Love*.
Let it grow
Let it multiply!

COMPANIONSHIP

Your steps radiate outward
Toward the one who is alone
Weary, without hope
Yet waiting in anticipation
Of your radiant smile
Your empathetic ear
Your willingness to listen.
Yes, in silence
You are the presence
Present to the other.
The welcome figure
In iridescent purple.
Yes, in silence
A geyser overflowing.
Cloaking with comfort
Quenching the loneliness
Quelling the gloom.
Warmth
issues forth
From your silent
Strengthening
Presence.
This is the road map
Of your heart.
Silent and strong
Giving to the other
What has been poured out on you -
Love

FACES TO LOVE

A formless heap
Meets my eye.
With a gasp
I jump back
Stop in my tracks
Take in the face
Buried under the throw.

The furrows of years
The creases of time
The raspy breath
The toothless smile.
Unkempt hair
Standing on edge
A prickly hedgehog
Enough to repel.

Stench fills the nostrils
Stale breath
Foul odor
Unhygienic through and through.
Breathing
At a standstill
Momentarily.
I hold my breath
Intermittently.

I must proceed
I cannot recede
There's no turning back.
I stretch out my hand.
With gentle strokes
Caress the forehead

And cheeks
Wipe away the rivulet
dripping down
The valley of the mouth.

The lights of the eyes
have dimmed
Strength has left
The limbs.
Movement
A veritable ordeal.

Fingers thumb the beads
Deliberate
Repetitive.
A glimmer
A spark
Fills the lanterns
Of the eyes.
A stream of tears
Flows down the cheeks.

Hail Mary
Full of Grace.
The words inaudible
Yet so distinct.
A whisper
An incomprehensible murmur
full of power.
Mesmerizing
All encompassing
Totally engulfing.

The chant grows
In unison.

AUTHENTICITY

Love flows
Unimpeded
Unencumbered.
Faith blooms in the furrows
Hope arises amidst the creases.
An outpouring of Grace
Perfumes
The decrepit body.

No need to recoil
Turn not away.
The mask is lifted
The disguise cast aside.
The flame burns bright
Forever living
Inextinguishable
Triumphant
Glorious
An encounter with Love.

GIVING

Thunderous downpour
                Deafening
                Gushing
                      Waterfall.

Face splashed
Sheet drenched
Clinging to soaked feet.
Eyes fixed
      On firework display
             In a chaotic sky.
Armageddon -

I cringe
Wrap the sheet tightly
Around me
As the hard
Wooden plank
Creaks
Crying in want
In pain.
The flood
Intensifies
Through
The gaping mouth
Of the wide iron bars
White flakes
Floating
To the floor
At the foot
Of the rigid
Hardwood
My bed.
Furrows on the wall

Crumbling plaster.

Cocooned
Fetal position.
Marooned.
Huis Clos.
A mound
Of bodies
On the floor.
Three generations
Oblivious
To the celestial
Opening
Of the flood gates -
Rhythmic breathing
Angelic expression
The granddaughters.

Guilt creeps
Walks stealthily
Over my wet
Cold feet
Advances
Into my limbs
My extremities
Heats my face
Overpowering.
How can I complain?
I occupy the place
Of honor
I rest on the throne.
The only place
Of comfort
In the confines
Of these sparse

Dilapidated
walls.
The yellowed
Photos
Pass before
My eyes.
The creaking stand
Of
Ancestral
Memories
Treasure Chest
Axis
Of
Rotation
Gravitational force
The matriarch
widow
grandmother
Holds out
Her parachute -
Huddled within
A paralyzed mother
two young daughters.
I am the outsider
Yet the one
In the center.

Lay bare
My conscience
Search
Question
Without reserve.
The response -
Every need
Met.

Catered to. . .
No lacuna
Nothing wanting. . .
"Reena,
I hear
The *bhaji wallah*.
Here, take these -
Rupees
Buy some
Palak,
Add to it
Some *Gobi*.
Make sure
It's fresh.
Tell Vishnu
We have
A guest.
He'll take care
Of the rest."
Shrikhand
Puri
Conjured up
With a wave
Of Anu's
Culinary wand.
"The least
I can do, Tai
Offer you
A platter of
My culinary
Delights."
Glow
Of Accomplishment
Rushes
Through

The face.
Bocuse
Of the
East.
Satisfies
Every
Palette
Indefatigable
With
Herculean
Mind
Heart
Hands.
Shriveled
Feet
Limp
Lifeless
An appendage
Disappear
Into
Nothingness.
No deprivation
Of
Local flavor.

Mounted on the back of Pegasus
Aji's
Two-wheeler
Kicking
Up dust
Flying high
Into
The smog
Potholes.
Meena

Upright
At the front
Reena
Straddling
The rear
Compact seat
I hang on
Hold my breath
She hugs
Grandmother
Aji
Queen
Of Jhansi
Charging
Into
The multitudinous
Foray.

Interlude
Juhu Beach
Bhel Puri
At
Chowpaty.
Salt
Pungent
Weighing heavily
In
The air.
Polluted
Waters
Arabian Sea
Evening strollers
Escaping
Steamy
Claustrophobic

Quarters
Find respite.
Marine Drive
The Queen's
Necklace.
Join
The melee
At Gateway
To
India.
Awestruck.
Taj Hotel
Looms
Ahead
2008 -
Sorcerous
Flames
Fan
Their
Forked tongues
Engulf
The
Palatial
Abode.
Evil
On the rampage
In an
Incandescent
Mumbai sky.
NIGHTMARE.
Bloody
Terrorist
Attacks
Horror
Reigns.

Last
Stop
Jehangir
Art Gallery
Haunting
Photography
Rajasthan
Drought
Riveting
Heart
Wrenching.
Pav Bhaji
For four
Aji
Calls out
In a
Strident voice
To the
Vendor
Pushing the
Hand cart.
A yearning
To cradle
The orphaned
Dog
Grips me.
Epitome
Of
Hunger
Eyes
Unfathomable
Pools
Penetrating
Pleading
Craving

For
Food
For
Love
Longing
To
Belong
Shooed away
With
A
Careless flick
Of
The hand.
"Here's
A chapati"
Aji whispers
Laying it
Into my hand
"Give it
To the mongrel"
I do
As
She says
Marveling
At her
Strong
Confident
Tone
Unflagging
Energy.
She commands
Expects to be
Followed
Yet. . .
Beneath

The facade
A softer
Gentler
Undertone
In her eyes
Glimpses
Of tenderness
No camouflage
The softness
Of
A warm
Fluffy
Kitten.
Search
My
Soul
Look
Within. . .
Peel away
The
Accoutrements
The
Core
Shines
A
Tree trunk
Rooted
Well-watered
Hospitality
Gushing
Fountain
Never ending
All
Encompassing

THE GIFT

The farmhouse on the promontory beckons,
its wide verandah calls
invitingly.
A welcome respite
from the scorching sun.
The stingers of the flaming ball
piercing the dermis,
the air heavy laden.
Chan, chan, kithi chan
Beautiful, magnificent, how wonderful!
The chant
echoes in unison,
rising from the dust
as the dirt covered van screeches to a grinding halt.

The good doctor and his Mrs.
hosts gracious,
overly polite.
Hear the whispering,
the murmur of the crowd -
So wealthy but oh so modest!
No airs about them!
Absolutely unassuming!
The host and hostess
wear pasted smiles.
The duo -
Peacock
Peahen
fan their feathers,
showcase their filigreed tails
in full glory.
Pride dances a jig,
builds momentum,

swells, reaches a crescendo.
dazzling;
mesmerizing.
With a flourish
The spectators are swept into the tour
of the country estate;
the castle.

Exclamations
Admiration
Acclamations
Accolades
Glowing remarks. . .
An architectural marvel!
The pride of the family.
Venue par excellence
of the homeopathic physicians' convention.
Our herbal garden
our acres of cultivated grounds. . .
My feet drag,
my mind drifts.

Laggard! I hear my name.
I've been looking for you.
Where have you been?
You were nowhere to be seen.
You missed out!
Jadhav Sahib's mango groves
as far as the eye can see;
an expanse of cashew trees
coconut palms stretching down to the Arabian Sea. . .

My eyes fall on the figures
silhouetted in the sunlight.
Barefooted,
Awkward,
Motionless,
Afraid. . .
to be discovered.
silently bearing
the heated vapors
rising from the
parched earth.
Teeth ravaged by
years of chewing
betel nuts,
a sparsely populated mouth
overshadowed by a ready smile
creasing into furrows
an open face.
Spontaneity,
without duplicity
no facade.
A mud shack
their dwelling.
The servants.
A folding of hands,
a sweeping bow
Hospitality personified.
Tea sweetened with jaggery
brewed on an outdoor fire,
served in charred tin mugs.
Bundya the dog
forever fastened,
seldom experiencing freedom,
insecure,
shudders and grunts

at the touch of my hands.
I feel the bones
under the taut skin.
Nuzzling but for a minute,
pulling back
afraid. . .to be loved.
Bai Sahib
What should I give you
as a token,
As a souvenir?
I have nothing,
nothing of value.
She stands before me
eyes downcast.
Bai Sahib, please accept this,
do not turn it down.
I offer it to you -
In her gnarled hands
she holds a sacred Tulsi plant.
Bai Sahib, a Tulsi plant
cultivated especially for you.
She gently marks my forehead
with *kumkum* and *haldi*.
In a barely audible voice
she whispers -
May it bring you peace
May it bring you joy.
The sacred plant
Lies in my lap
Drenched in tears.
Rukhmini's most prized possession.

Made in the USA
Monee, IL
15 February 2020

21846012R00033